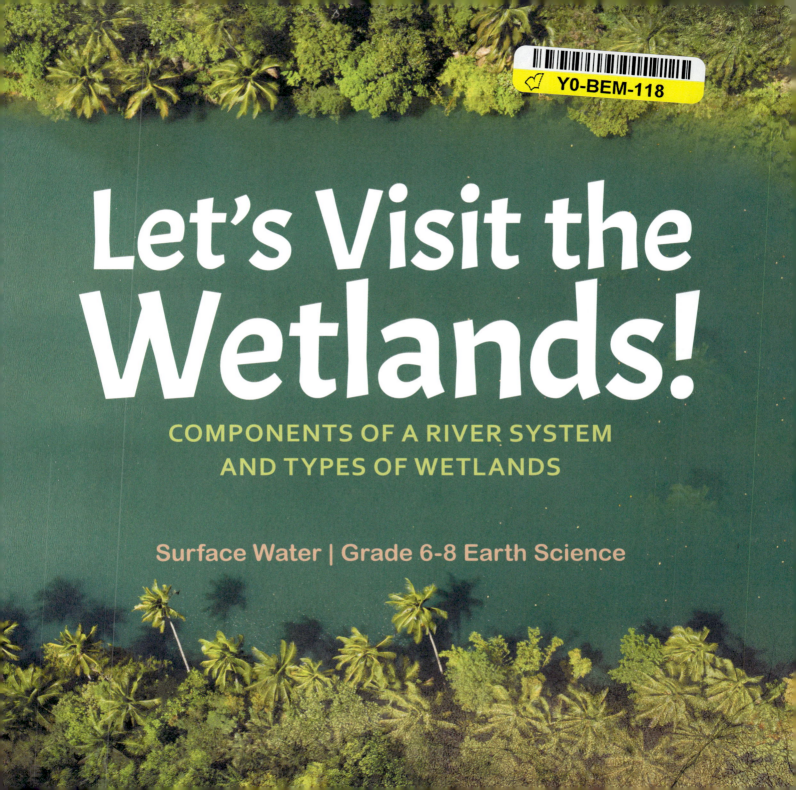

Let's Visit the Wetlands!

COMPONENTS OF A RIVER SYSTEM AND TYPES OF WETLANDS

Surface Water | Grade 6-8 Earth Science

BABY PROFESSOR
EDUCATION KIDS

First Edition, 2024

Published in the United States by Speedy Publishing LLC, 40 E Main Street, Newark, Delaware 19711 USA.

© 2024 Baby Professor Books, an imprint of Speedy Publishing LLC

Baby Professor Books are available at special discounts when purchased in bulk for industrial and sales-promotional use. For details contact our Special Sales Team at Speedy Publishing LLC, 40 E Main Street, Newark, Delaware 19711 USA. Telephone (888) 248-4521 Fax: (210) 519-4043.

10 9 8 7 6 * 5 4 3 2 1

Print Edition: 9781541990470
Digital Edition: 9781541991835
Hardcover Edition: 9781541989511

See the world in pictures. Build your knowledge in style.
www.speedypublishing.com

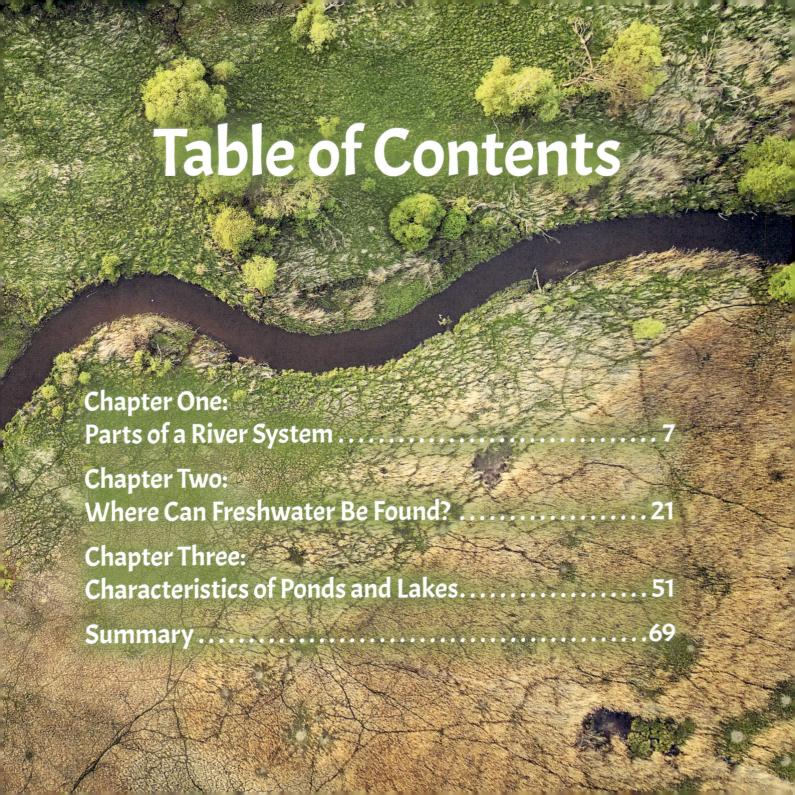

Table of Contents

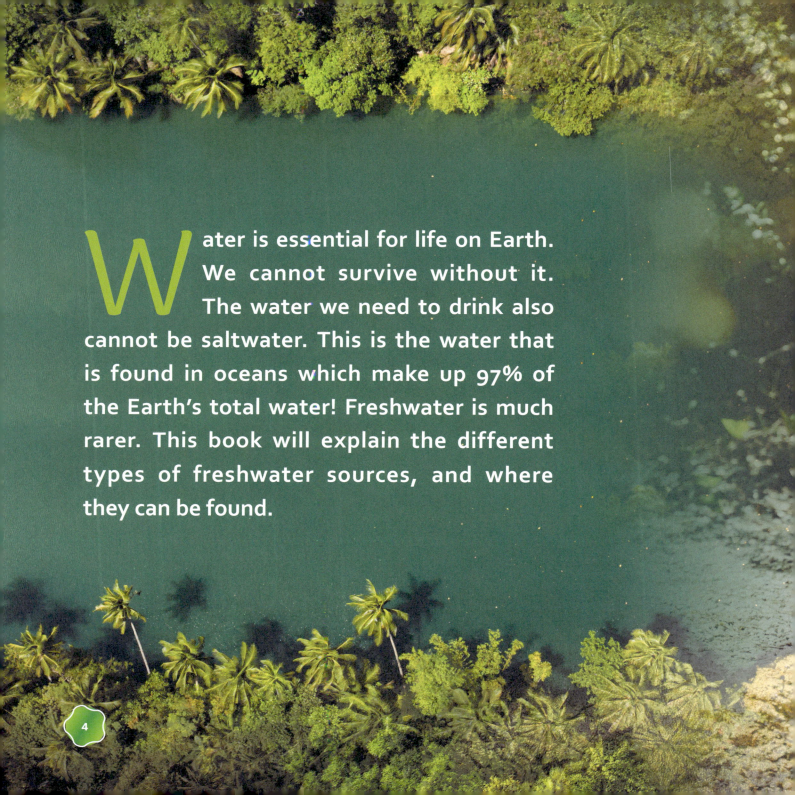

Water is essential for life on Earth. We cannot survive without it. The water we need to drink also cannot be saltwater. This is the water that is found in oceans which make up 97% of the Earth's total water! Freshwater is much rarer. This book will explain the different types of freshwater sources, and where they can be found.

6

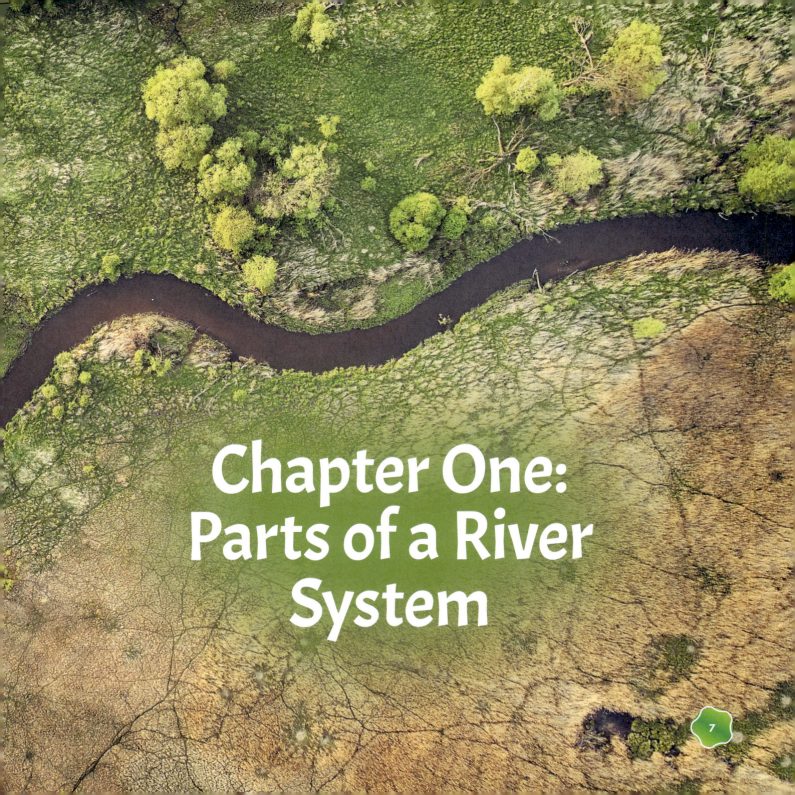

Chapter One: Parts of a River System

Rivers are an excellent and important source of freshwater.

Rivers are an excellent and important source of freshwater. Many of the first civilizations began along rivers. There are many parts to rivers.

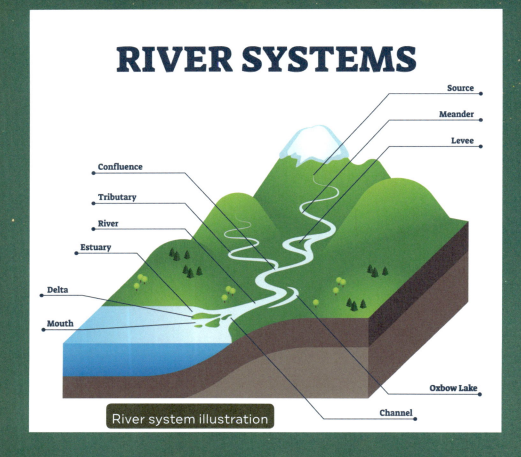

RIVER SYSTEMS

Source
Meander
Levee
Confluence
Tributary
River
Estuary
Delta
Mouth
Oxbow Lake
Channel

River system illustration

What is a River System?

Water moves from areas of high elevation to low elevation. Rivers tend to start at the top of mountains. From there, runoff runs along the ground and accumulates into streams. Runoff is rainwater or melted snow that is not absorbed by the ground.

These small streams will combine with other streams. Then, these streams will flow into small rivers. These small rivers will then form into larger rivers. These rivers that flow into larger rivers are called tributaries. Rivers and their tributaries make up what is called river systems.

Tributaries of river Beas flowing from the high mountains at Manali, Himachal Pradesh, India.

Watersheds:

A watershed is an area of land that provides the water to a river system. Drainage basins are another name for watersheds. It can help to remember that water is shed from the land after it rains or as snow melts. This runoff is what fills the rivers. Water can also be channeled into soil, groundwater, creeks, ponds and lakes.

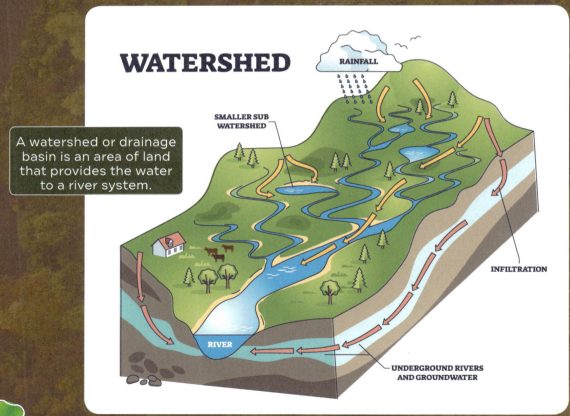

A watershed or drainage basin is an area of land that provides the water to a river system.

The Tahquamenon River watershed as it empties into Lake Superior, Tahquamenon Falls State Park, Paradise, Michigan.

Watersheds can be small or large. They might only have a few acres, or they can cover enough land that water drains into bays or oceans.

An example of a large watershed is Chesapeake Bay. This is a large area of water. It connects to the Atlantic Ocean. The Atlantic Ocean is on the eastern coast of North America. This bay is located in Maryland and Virginia. Its watershed covers or touches various parts of six different states and Washington DC. It has more than 100,000 tributaries! Some of the tributaries are, in fact, large rivers. The Chesapeake Bay is one of the largest watersheds in the United States.

Chesapeake Bay is one of the largest watersheds in the U.S.

How are Watersheds Separated?

Watersheds are divided by ridges. These ridges are aptly named divides. A ridge is merely an area that has higher elevation. These ridges are above sea level. Water can run down both sides of these ridges.

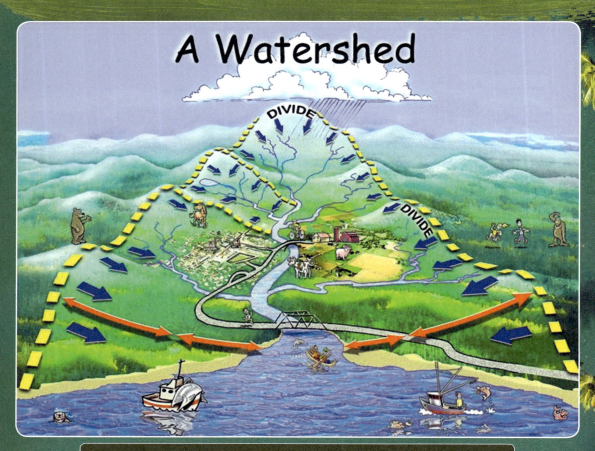

Watersheds are divided by ridges which are aptly named divides.

Panorama of the Great Carpathian Water Dividing Ridge in Ukraine.

The water that flows down the opposite sides also flows in opposite directions and towards different bodies of water. The water from each side goes to different regions. Hence, the ridges divide the watershed.

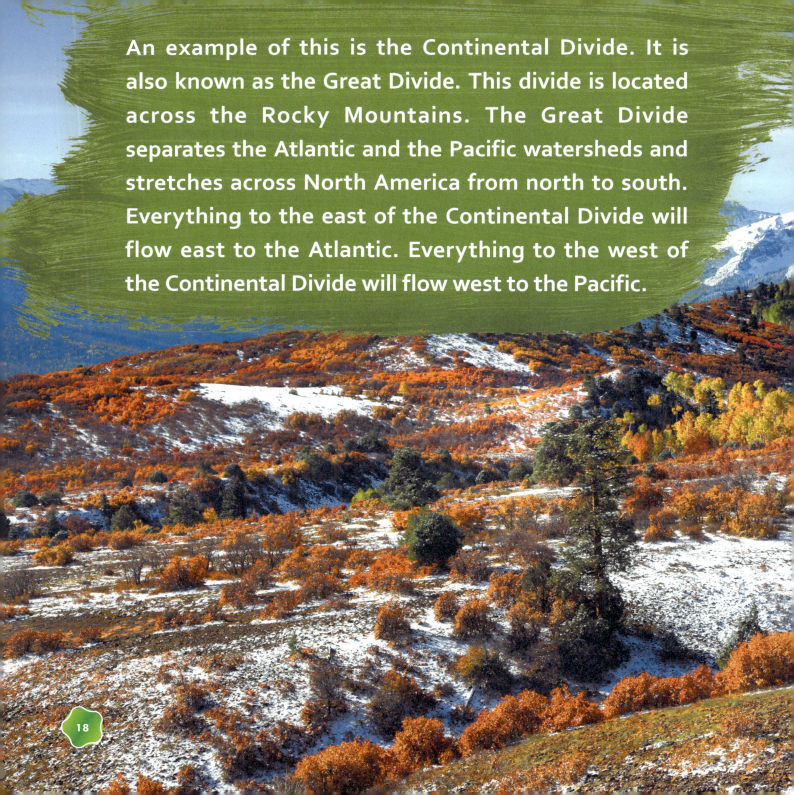

An example of this is the Continental Divide. It is also known as the Great Divide. This divide is located across the Rocky Mountains. The Great Divide separates the Atlantic and the Pacific watersheds and stretches across North America from north to south. Everything to the east of the Continental Divide will flow east to the Atlantic. Everything to the west of the Continental Divide will flow west to the Pacific.

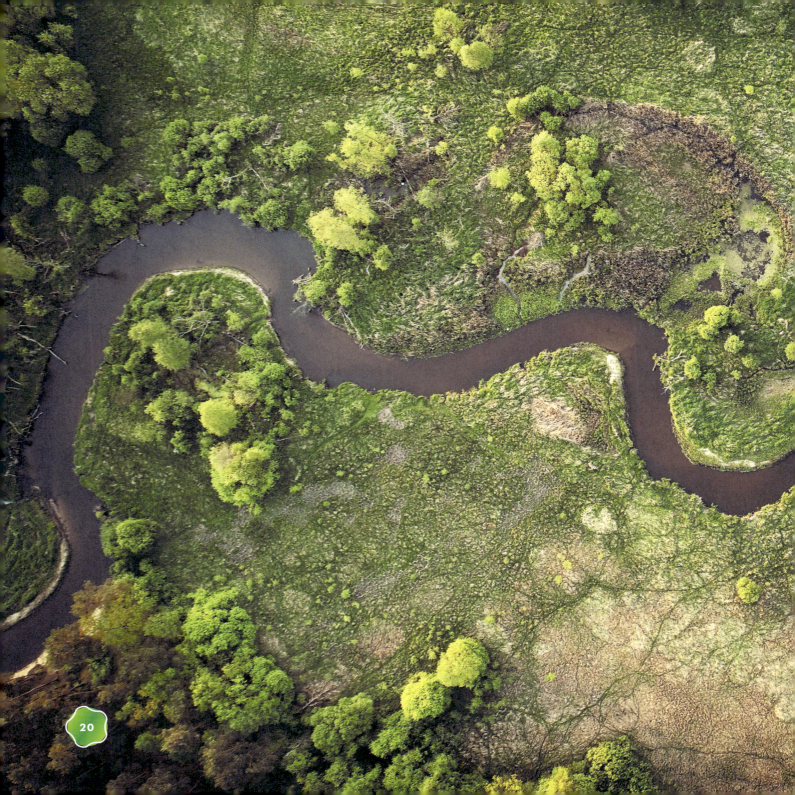

Chapter Two: Where Can Freshwater Be Found?

Freshwater is found in rivers, groundwater, water vapor, lakes, and even ice sheets.

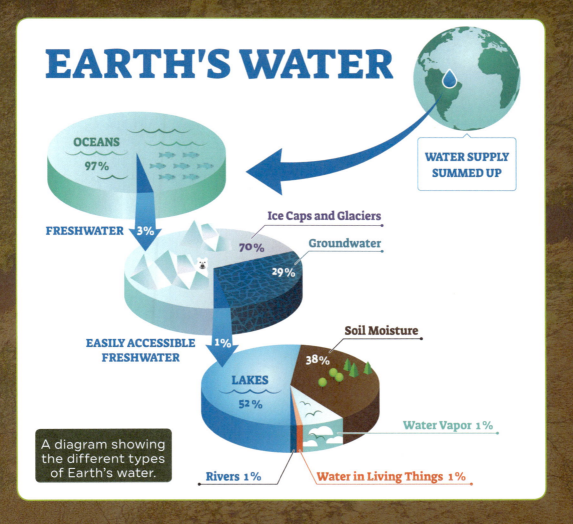

EARTH'S WATER

WATER SUPPLY SUMMED UP

OCEANS 97%

FRESHWATER 3%

Ice Caps and Glaciers 70%

Groundwater 29%

EASILY ACCESSIBLE FRESHWATER 1%

Soil Moisture 38%

LAKES 52%

Water Vapor 1%

Rivers 1%

Water in Living Things 1%

A diagram showing the different types of Earth's water.

River systems are not the only sources of freshwater on Earth. It is also found in groundwater, water vapor, lakes, and even ice sheets. In fact, 75% of freshwater on Earth is frozen! The other 25% is mostly found underground. Tiny amounts of freshwater can also be found in the atmosphere as vapor.

Ice Sheets:

Ice sheets are an area of glacial land ice. They extend more than 20,000 square miles. They are long and flat.

Ice sheet near Kangerlussuaq, Greenland.

Today, the largest ice sheets that can be found on Earth are in Greenland and Antarctica. They cover most of these two areas. These ice sheets are found near the two poles.

During the last ice age, ice sheets were more frequent and farther away from the poles. They covered most of Scandinavia and North America.

Ice Sheets in Lofoten, Nordland, Norway.

When ice sheets break apart, the pieces can become icebergs. These icebergs will gradually melt as they drift into warmer waters.

Ground Water:

Groundwater is found underneath the surface of the Earth. When people dig wells, they are digging to reach groundwater. Groundwater accumulates as gravity brings water down through the soil and rocks. This water comes from rain and melted snow. Groundwater fills the spaces between the various particles and broken rock fragments.

Groundwater is found underneath the surface of the Earth.

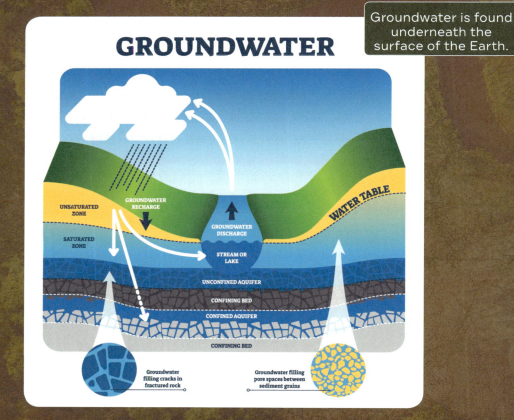

When people dig wells, they are digging to reach groundwater.

Just slightly over half of the population of the United States drink groundwater. Almost all of these people who rely on groundwater live in rural areas. Rural areas are areas out in the country. For example, people who live on farms live in a rural area. The opposite of rural is urban. Urban life is city life.

Just slightly over half of the population of the U.S. drink groundwater.

Groundwater helps provide irrigation.

Groundwater is critical for farming. It helps provide irrigation. Groundwater also feeds into other bodies of water like lakes or rivers. This keeps them supplied with water.

31

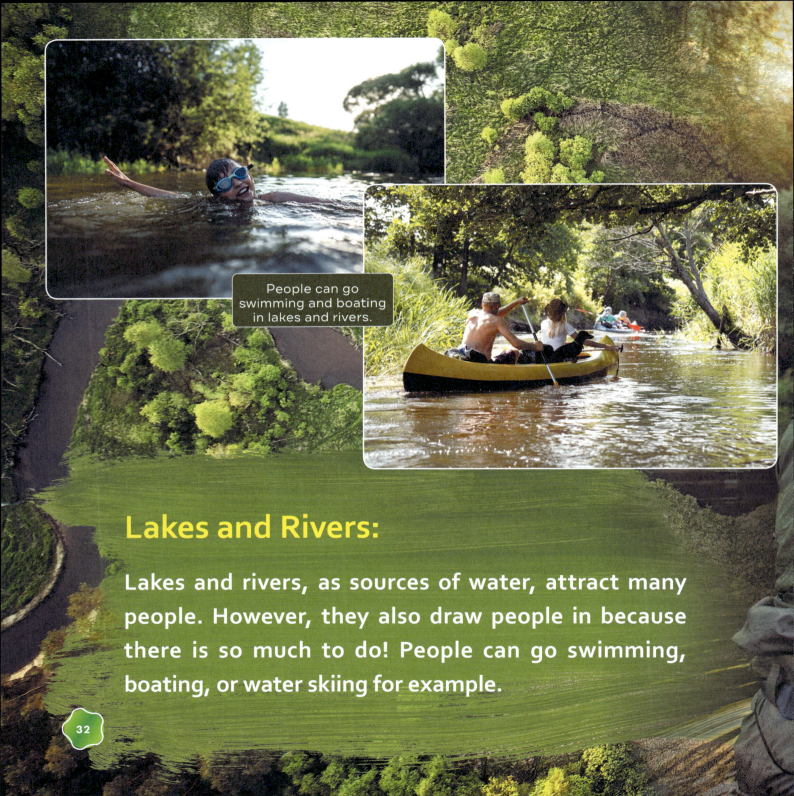

People can go swimming and boating in lakes and rivers.

Lakes and Rivers:

Lakes and rivers, as sources of water, attract many people. However, they also draw people in because there is so much to do! People can go swimming, boating, or water skiing for example.

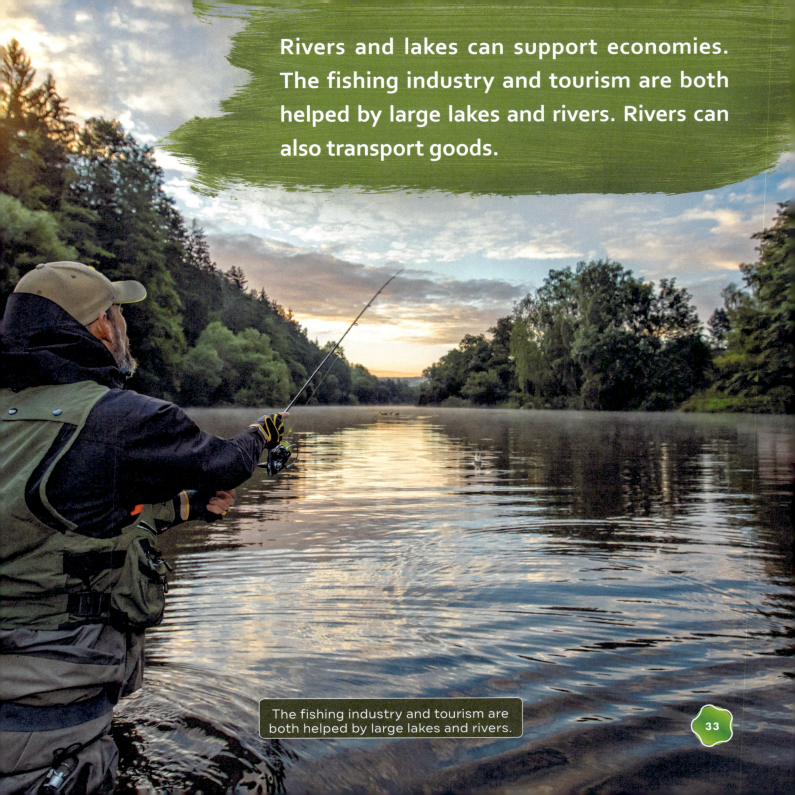

Rivers and lakes can support economies. The fishing industry and tourism are both helped by large lakes and rivers. Rivers can also transport goods.

The fishing industry and tourism are both helped by large lakes and rivers.

The Great Lakes are massive lakes. They contain about 20% of the freshwater on the Earth's surface. This means they contribute a lot to freshwater stores.

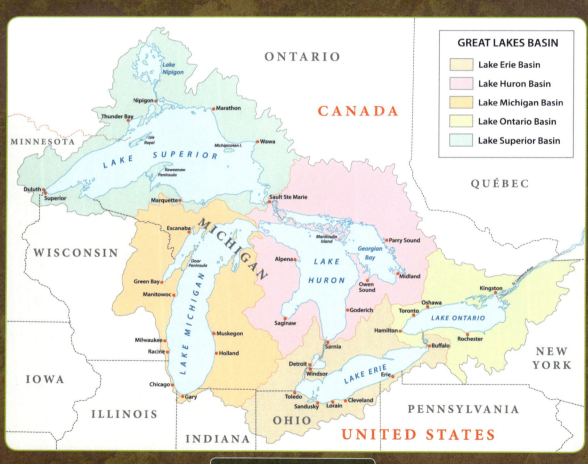

GREAT LAKES BASIN
- Lake Erie Basin
- Lake Huron Basin
- Lake Michigan Basin
- Lake Ontario Basin
- Lake Superior Basin

Map of the Great Lakes

Just slightly smaller than the Great Lakes, the United States also has Lake Tahoe. This is the deepest lake in the world. These lakes provide drinking water and nutrition for plants, animals, and fish.

Emerald Bay, Lake Tahoe, California

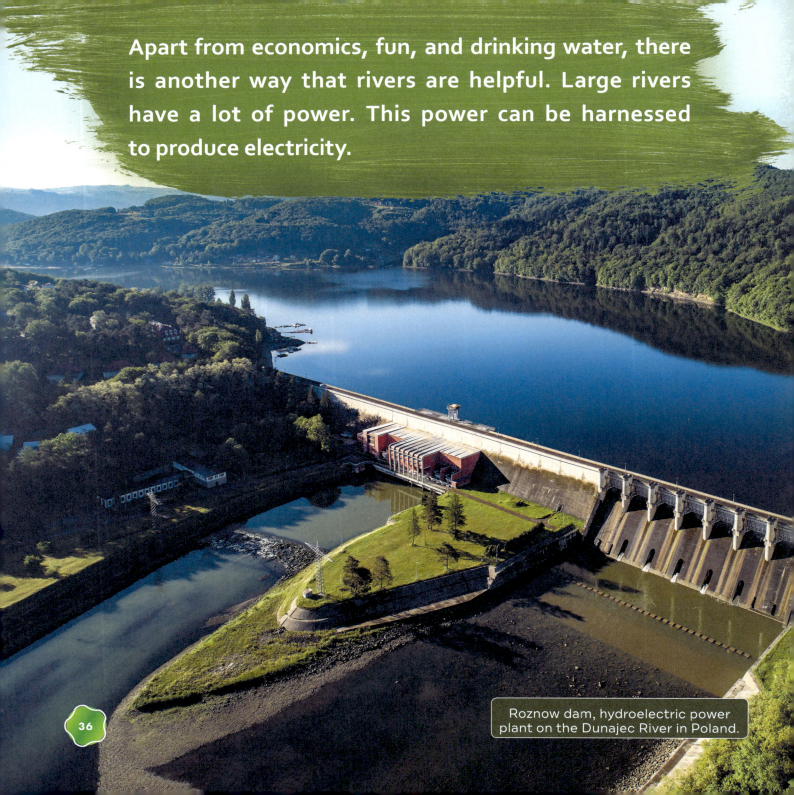

Apart from economics, fun, and drinking water, there is another way that rivers are helpful. Large rivers have a lot of power. This power can be harnessed to produce electricity.

Roznow dam, hydroelectric power plant on the Dunajec River in Poland.

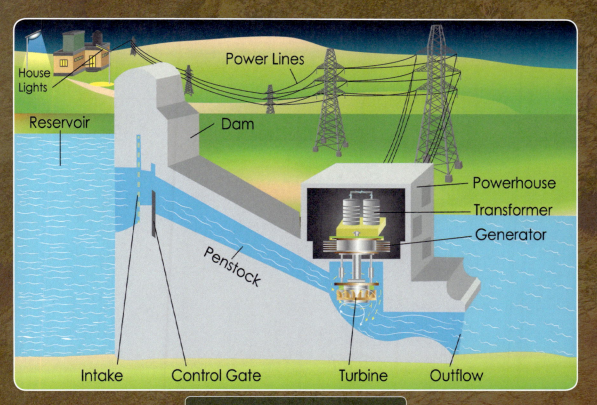

House Lights

Power Lines

Reservoir

Dam

Powerhouse

Transformer

Generator

Penstock

Intake   Control Gate   Turbine   Outflow

Illustration of hydropower plant.

Hydroelectric dams are built at rivers. They use the movement of the water to turn turbines. This generates hydroelectricity, or electricity produced using the energy of water.

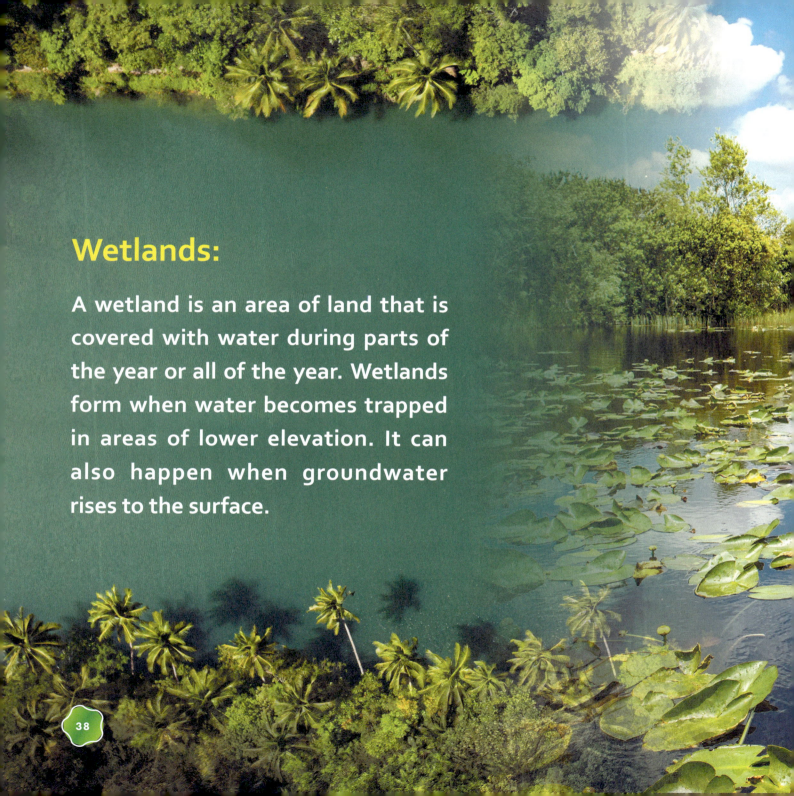

Wetlands:

A wetland is an area of land that is covered with water during parts of the year or all of the year. Wetlands form when water becomes trapped in areas of lower elevation. It can also happen when groundwater rises to the surface.

Florida wetland at Everglades National Park.

39

Wetlands are considered important, and many people are working to protect them. A vital reason to protect wetlands is that they filter water. In other words, they help improve water quality. They can even help reduce man-made pollution.

Okavango Wetlands at Okavango Delta, UNESCO World Heritage Site, Ramsar Wetland, Botswana, Africa.

41

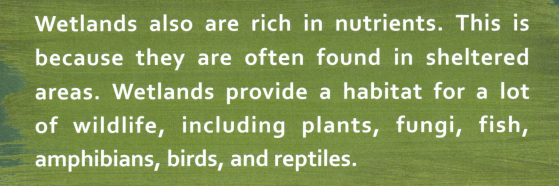

Wetlands also are rich in nutrients. This is because they are often found in sheltered areas. Wetlands provide a habitat for a lot of wildlife, including plants, fungi, fish, amphibians, birds, and reptiles.

Great Blue Heron in Wetland Habitat in Alberta, Canada.

Wetlands can help maintain the flow of surface water during dry periods.

Finally, wetlands can help maintain the flow of surface water during dry periods. On the other hand, they can also help control flooding.

The plants that live in marshes are mostly grass.

Freshwater wetlands come in three types: Marshes, swamps, and bogs. Marshes are grassy wetlands. You may have guessed that the plants that live in marshes are mostly grass. They are covered with a stream or shallow waters. Marshes are usually found near lakes or large rivers. They sort of bridge the gap between land and water.

44

Swamps look more like flooded forests. They tend to be found in water climates with more humidity.

Swamps look more like flooded forests.

Last of all, there are bogs. These are found in the north where it is cooler. Bogs are quite acidic which make them a good environment for moss to grow in. A lot of bogs were formed in the depressions left by ice sheets.

Bogs are quite acidic which make them a good environment for moss to grow in.

Not all wetlands are freshwater wetlands though. Some wetlands form along the coasts of oceans and seas. Some coastal wetlands will form as a mix of salt and fresh water.

Coastal wetlands in the Natural Reserve Darßer Ort, Mecklenburg-Vorpommern, Germany.

Tha Pom Klong Song Nam mangrove forest or Emerald pool mangrove forest at Krabi, Thailand.

These coastal wetlands include things like forests of mangrove trees and salt marshes. Mangrove trees are unique. They have vast systems of roots, and they live both below and above the water!

Coastal wetlands also help to prevent flooding. They carry water similar to the way that sponges do. The plants in wetlands also help to prevent erosion by holding the sand together with their roots. Additionally, they prevent erosion by absorbing the energy from waves. This protects habitats that are further inland.

The plants in wetlands also help to prevent erosion by holding the sand together with their roots.

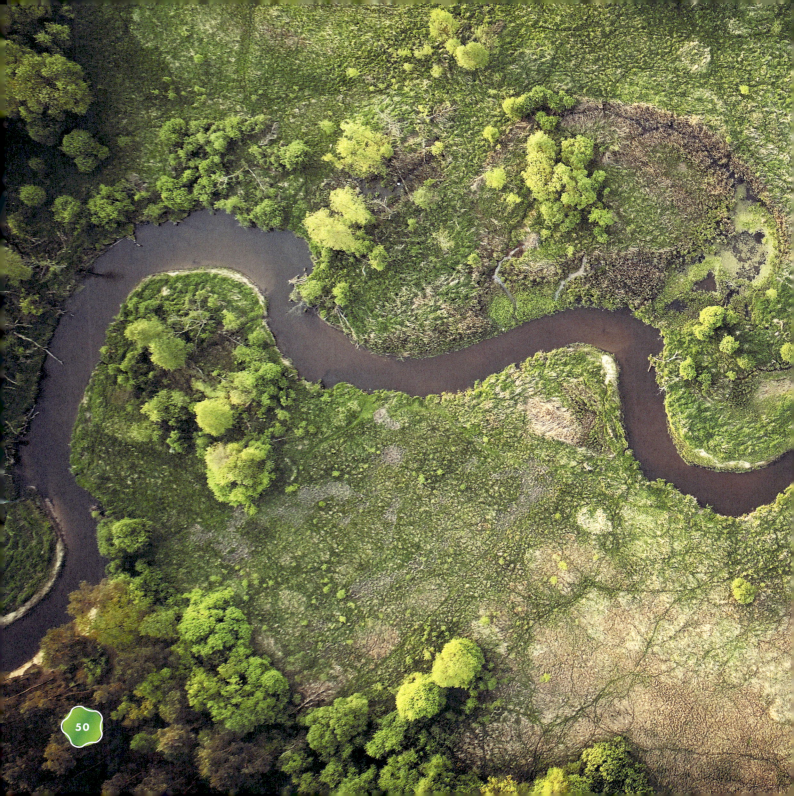

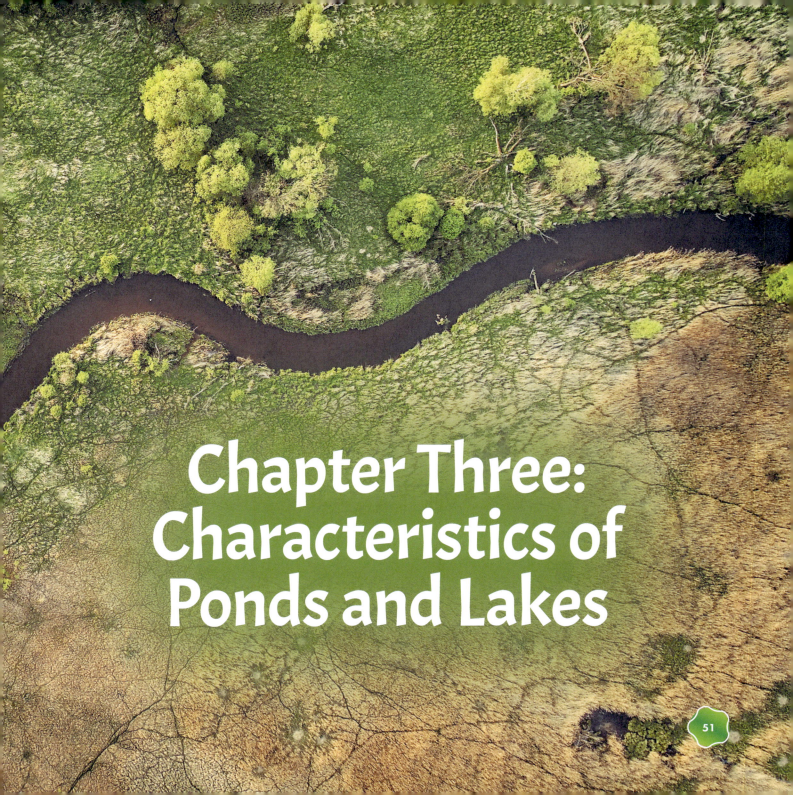

Chapter Three: Characteristics of Ponds and Lakes

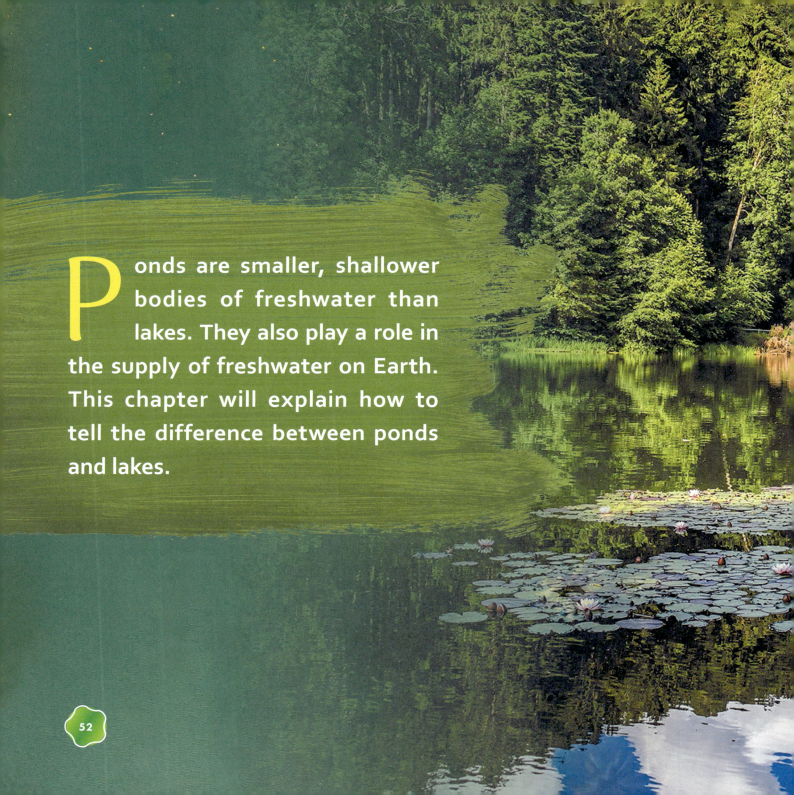

Ponds are smaller, shallower bodies of freshwater than lakes. They also play a role in the supply of freshwater on Earth. This chapter will explain how to tell the difference between ponds and lakes.

Ponds are smaller, shallower bodies of freshwater than lakes.

53

Plant growth is common throughout ponds.

Ponds, Lakes, Depth, and Sunlight:

Ponds tend to be both smaller and shallower than lakes. This means that sunlight will typically reach the bottom of a pond. Plant growth is common throughout ponds as a result.

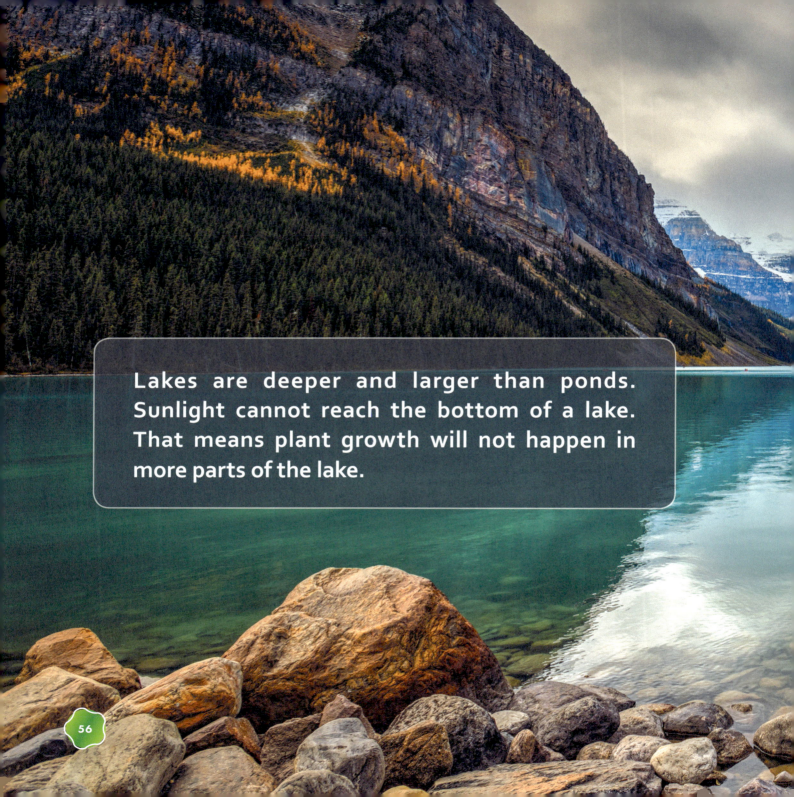

Lakes are deeper and larger than ponds. Sunlight cannot reach the bottom of a lake. That means plant growth will not happen in more parts of the lake.

Lake Louise in Banff National Park in the Rocky Mountains of Alberta, Canada.

Lack of plants also means fewer creatures living in the deep parts of the lake. There is nothing there to be eaten. Also, the water will be colder and darker.

How Ponds and Lakes Form:

Ponds form when melted snow and fallen rain collect in shallow, low-lying places. Sometimes they are also filled by groundwater or rivers. Typically though, this is just from rainfall collecting. Water may also flow out of a pond, and it is easy for ponds to completely evaporate too.

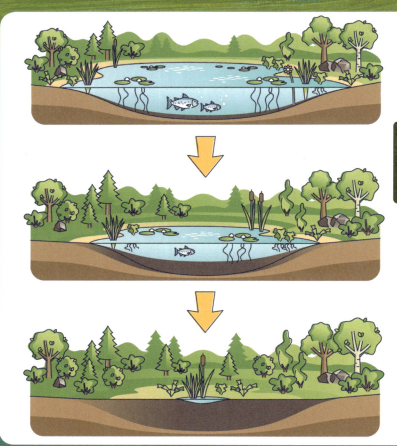

Diagram of aquatic succession and ecological pond drying process stages.

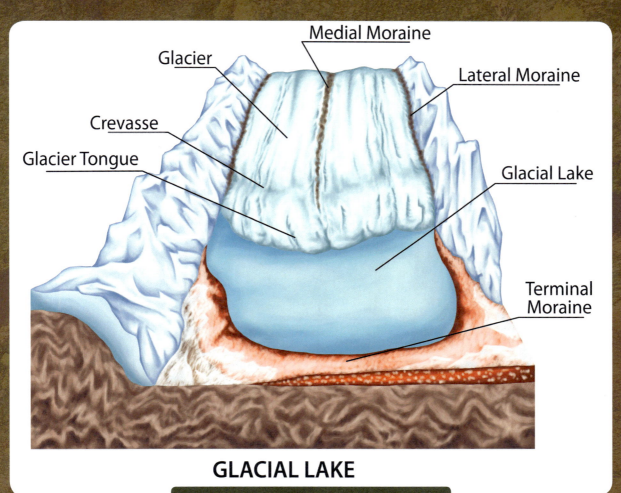

GLACIAL LAKE

Some of the depressions that form lakes are formed by ice sheets that melted.

Lakes can also form the way ponds do with water collecting in low areas. Some of the depressions that form lakes are formed by ice sheets that melted. This is how the Great Lakes were formed.

Nainital Lake in Kumaon, Uttarakhand, India, is a natural freshwater body formed by tectonics.

Another way lakes can form is from the movement of tectonic plates. For instance, areas where two plates pull apart can create natural depressions. These depressions can fill up with water.

TECTONIC LAKE

Block Mountains

Tectonic Lake

Slope Deposits

Alluvial Fan

Graben

Fault

Another way lakes can form is from the movement of tectonic plates.

Sometimes mud flows or lava flows from volcanoes erupting can block rivers. This creates a natural dam which blocks off the water. The result is a new lake. Sometimes dams can be man-made. A lake made by people is called a reservoir. An example of this kind of lake is Lake Mead. It is the largest reservoir in the United States. It was created in 1933 when the Hoover Dam was built.

Lake Mead, Grand Canyon Hoover Dam, Las Vegas, Nevada

63

Bonus Content

The Water Cycle

The water cycle is how water moves through the oceans, land, and air. All the water we use will go through this cycle and return to where it came from. In fact, the water that we drink has been going through this cycle for many centuries.

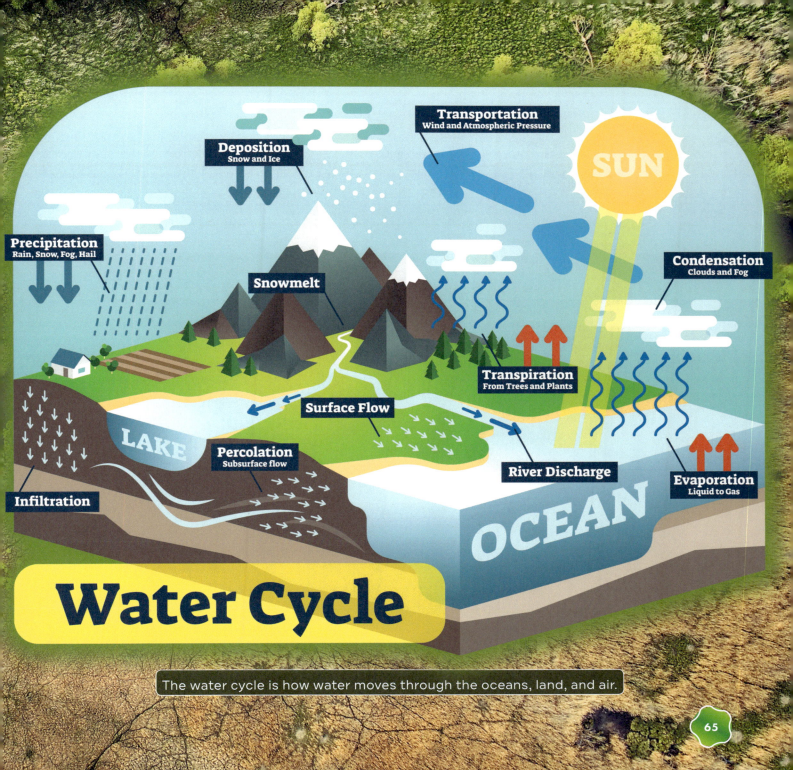

The water cycle is how water moves through the oceans, land, and air.

As the temperature cools, the water vapor condenses and forms clouds.

The water cycle starts with the evaporation of surface water. The water becomes vapor and moves into the atmosphere. As the temperature cools, the water vapor condenses. It forms clouds. Eventually, the water falls back to the ground as precipitation.

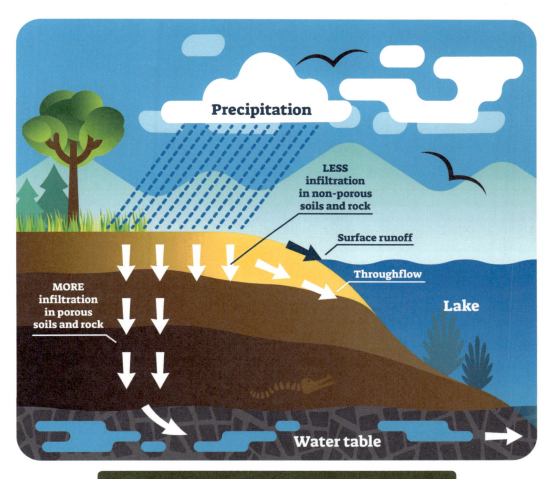

Precipitation

LESS infiltration in non-porous soils and rock

Surface runoff

Throughflow

Lake

MORE infiltration in porous soils and rock

Water table

The precipitation can become groundwater or runoff.

The precipitation can become groundwater or runoff. It can fill up ponds and lakes. The runoff flows down to enter river systems. These river systems empty into the oceans. When this water evaporates, the cycle starts again.

Summary

Freshwater only makes up about three percent of all the Earth's water. Even then, liquid freshwater can be hard to find on the Earth's surface. 75% of freshwater lies frozen in ice sheets. Much of the rest is found below the surface as groundwater. On the surface, freshwater is found in places like ponds, wetlands, lakes, and river systems. These areas of water not only provide drinkable water, but can also provide a place to live for some creatures, and can provide electricity or help sustain economies. Watersheds are areas of land that provide the water to river systems. They are separated by ridges as water moves from an area of high elevation to low elevation.

Visit

www.speedypublishing.com

To view and download free content on your
favorite subject and browse our catalog of new
and exciting books for readers of all ages.

Made in United States
Troutdale, OR
06/21/2024

20699897R00045